Contents

OXFORD
UNIVERSITY PRESS

This book belongs to

....

OXFORD
UNIVERSITY PRESS

Great Clarendon Street, Oxford, OX2 6DP, United Kingdom

Oxford University Press is a department of the University
of Oxford. It furthers the University's objective of excellence
in research, scholarship, and education by publishing worldwide.
Oxford is a registered trade mark of Oxford University Press
in the UK and in certain other countries

British Library Cataloguing in Publication Data
Data available

ISBN: 978-0-19-277380-7

10 9 8 7 6 5 4 3 2 1

Paper used in the production of this book is a natural, recyclable product made from
wood grown in sustainable forests. The manufacturing process conforms to the
environmental regulations of the country of origin.

Printed in China

Acknowledgements

Series Editor: Nikki Gamble

How this collection works

This collection offers six funny, action-packed, heart-warming and thought-provoking stories to engage your child and encourage reading progression. The stories are specially written to support and develop your child's growing reading skills, and are fully in line with the phonics your child is learning at school.

How to use this book

Reading should be a shared and enjoyable experience for both you and your child. Pick a time when your child is not distracted by other things, and when they are happy to concentrate for about 15 minutes. Let them choose one or two of the stories for each reading session, so that they don't get too tired.

Read the tips on the next page, as they offer ideas and suggestions for getting the most out of this collection.

Tips for reading the stories together

Step 1 — Look together at the title page for each story before your child starts to read. What does your child think the story will be about? Use clues from the title and picture and talk about what might happen.

Step 2 — Ask your child to read the story out loud. Encourage them to stop and look at the pictures, and talk about what they are reading — either during the reading session, or afterwards. Your child will be able to read most of the words in the story, but if they struggle with a word, remind them to say the sounds in the word from left to right and then blend the sounds together to read the word, e.g. *c-r-a-ck-i-ng, cracking.* If they come across a tricky word that they cannot sound out, simply read the word to your child, e.g. *I, the, no.*

Step 3 — When your child has finished reading the story, discuss it together. Then turn to the fun activities at the end. These will help your child think and talk about what they have read.

The Dinosaur King

Written by Isabel Thomas

Illustrated by Steve Brown

Tops was cracking nuts. She felt
a bump on her horn.

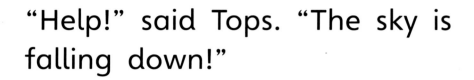

"Help!" said Tops. "The sky is falling down!"

"I must tell the Dinosaur King," she said.

To the Dinosaur King →

Tops set off to see the Dinosaur King.

Tops met Steg.

"The sky is falling down!" said Tops.
"I am off to tell the Dinosaur King."

"I will come, too," said Steg.

To the Dinosaur King →

Tops and Steg met Comp.

"The sky is falling down!" said Tops.
"We are off to tell the Dinosaur King."

"I will come, too," said Comp.

To the Dinosaur King →

Tops, Steg and Comp
went across a bog.

They went up a hill.

They got to the lair of
the Dinosaur King.

To the
Dinosaur
King →

"Come in," said the Dinosaur King.
"Sit next to me."

He was planning to munch the little dinosaurs for lunch!

Just then there was
a big **CRASH!**

"The sky *was* falling down,"
said Comp.

"I was right!" said Tops.

"Shall we go back and look for nuts?"
said Steg.

Talk about it!

What fell on me at the start of the story?

Who went with me to see the Dinosaur King?

Do you think the Dinosaur King deserved what happened at the end? Why?

Put them in order!

Write numbers 1 to 5 to show the order these pictures come in the story. The first one has been done for you.

1

Planet Cake

Written by Teresa Heapy

Illustrated by Ana García

Beth had a rocket.

"I am going to visit a different planet!" she said.

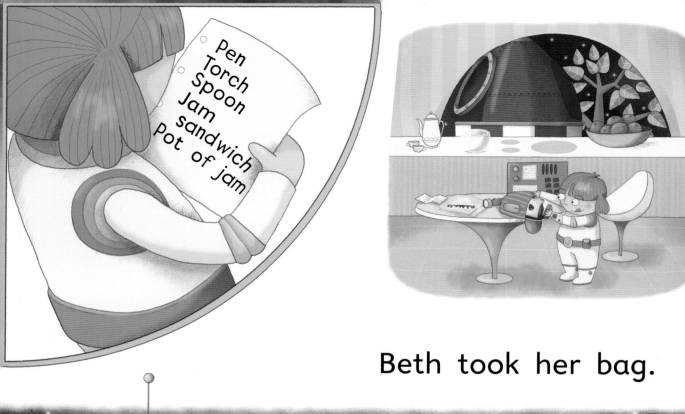

Beth took her bag.

She put on her helmet.
She got into her rocket.

The rocket shot
into the sky.

It landed
on a planet.

THUMP!

29

Beth got out.

"There are just rocks on this planet," she said.

30

"Not just rocks," said a Cake-bot.
"They are rock *cakes*."

"Hmm," said Beth. "This cake is a bit dry."

"*What?*" said the Cake-bot.

"I think this cake needs some ... **jam**!" said Beth.

Beth split the rock cake.
She put some jam on it.

34

"There!" said Beth.

"Have a bit."

"**Mmmm!**" said the Cake-bot. "It's good!"

Beth and the Cake-bot put jam on lots of cakes.

"That is a **big** cake!" said Beth.

"Thank you," said the Cake-bot.

Beth got back into her rocket.

Beth was back on her planet.

"I can see Planet Cake!" she said.

Talk about it!

What was odd about the rocks on Planet Cake?

What useful thing did I have in my bag?

Who do you think will eat all the cakes on Planet Cake?

Unscramble the letters

Unscramble the letters to make words from the story.

telhem _____

ckoret _____

lentap _____

Ceka-otb _____

theB _____

The Lark
and the Owl

Written by Paul Shipton

Illustrated by Jenny Løvlie

The night was black.

"I am afraid," said the lark.

An owl swept across the dark sky.

Then the owl landed next to the lark.

"You must not be afraid
of the night," said the owl.

"I can help you," said the owl.
"Will you come with me now?"

"Yes," said the lark.

Up in the dark sky, the owl hooted
at the moon and the stars.

The sun began to come up.

The sky got lighter and lighter.
The owl was afraid.

The owl began to fly back to the cool, dark forest.

"You must not be afraid of the light," said the lark. "Will you come with me?"

"Yes," said the owl.

Up they went in the clear, bright sky.

The owl felt the sunlight on her wings.

The lark sang to the morning sun.

Soon, the sunlight was too strong.
The owl went back to the forest.

But now, the owl always waits to meet the lark at dawn.

Good morning!

And at sunset, the lark always waits to wish the owl goodnight.

Goodnight!

Talk about it!

What was I afraid of?

What was the owl afraid of?

Were the owl and I friends in the end? How do you know?

Match the rhymes

Draw lines to match each word to the bird it rhymes with! One example has been done for you.

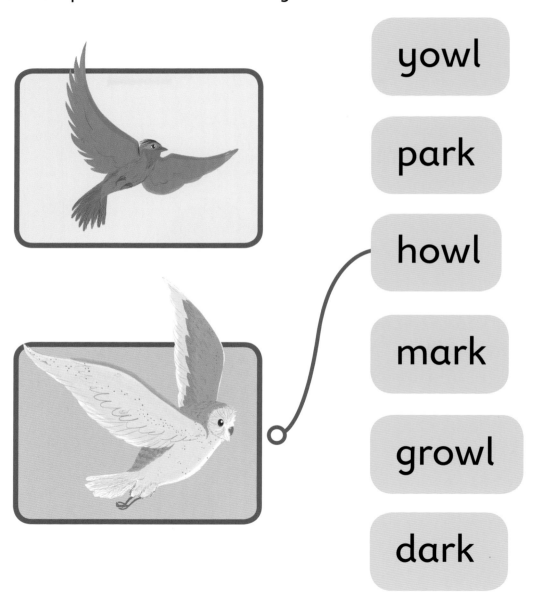

yowl

park

howl

mark

growl

dark

Snoot's Birthday Surprise

Written by Simon Puttock

Illustrated by Thomas Docherty

"It's my birthday soon," said Snoot.

"I know," said Milton. "It's my birthday, too, on the same day."

"Do you know what I would like for a present?" said Snoot.
"I can tell you if you want."

"You don't need to tell me," said Milton. "I'm sure I can think of something."

Later, Snoot saw Milton out shopping.

"Are you sure you don't need any help choosing my present?" Snoot said.

"No, thank you," said Milton.

The next day, Snoot saw Milton.
"I want to tell you something," he said.

"What is it?" said Milton.

"I don't want lots of presents for my birthday," said Snoot. "I just want one **special** present, please."

"That is not a problem," said Milton.

The next day, Snoot went to see Milton again.

"I forgot to ask," said Snoot. "What do *you* want for *your* birthday, Milton?"

Bicycles are best! Yellow ones are better!

Milton thought for a moment.

"I'd like a surprise, please," he said.

Snoot tried to think of a present for Milton but the only thing he could think of was a bicycle.

But Milton already had a bicycle.
It was blue, with fancy wheels.

At last, Snoot had an idea.

He would *make* something for Milton. But what could he make?

"I know," thought Snoot,
"I will start making it,
and when it is finished
I will know what it is!"

75

Snoot got lots of stuff,
tape and glue. He spent
all morning making something.

When he was done, he still didn't know what it was.

But it *was* surprising.

The special day arrived.

"Happy birthday, Snoot!" said Milton.

"Happy birthday, Milton!" said Snoot.
"This is for you!"

Milton opened his present.

"Wow!" said Milton. "It's very surprising! Thank you. But what is it?"

"I have no idea," said Snoot.

"I love it anyway," said Milton.

"Now I have a present for you,"
said Milton.

He gave Snoot a piece of string.

"Oh," said Snoot, trying not to look disappointed. "It's string. Thank you. It's lovely."

"Don't be silly, Snoot," said Milton.
"The string is not your present! To find
your present, follow the string!"

"How exciting!" said Snoot.

And he followed the string until ...

... "Surprise!" said Milton.

"That is just what I wanted!" said Snoot.
"How did you guess?"

Talk about it!

How did I try to let Milton know what I wanted for my birthday?

Why did I feel disappointed at first, when Milton gave me my present?

How did Milton feel about the present I made him?

YELLOW BIKE WEEKLY

Choose the right words

Read the sentences. Write the correct word in each gap.

1. Snoot wanted a _____ bicycle. (blue, red, yellow)

2. Milton wanted a _____. (bicycle, surprise, skateboard)

3. Snoot _____ a present for Milton. (made, borrowed, bought)

4. Snoot _____ the present Milton gave him. (hated, loved, broke)

Bicycle maze

Draw a line to help Snoot find the yellow bicycle.

Snoot and Milton word search

Find the words in the grid.

s	b	i	c	y	c	l	e
u	g	y	e	l	l	o	w
r	h	j	a	i	q	z	s
p	k	m	i	l	t	o	n
r	s	d	x	u	w	l	o
i	n	o	r	i	m	v	o
s	p	r	e	s	e	n	t
e	p	a	d	b	o	k	f

Snoot   Milton   yellow

bicycle   surprise   present

The Night Knight

Written by Timothy Knapman

Illustrated by Steve May

It was the middle of the night but Jake couldn't sleep.

Then something,
somewhere, went **bump!**

"Help!" said Jake. "I'm scared!"

There was a flash and suddenly ...

... there was a knight in Jake's bedroom. He looked very brave.

"I am the Night Knight!" he said.
"I look after children when it's dark."

Then something,
somewhere, went **bump** again.

"Help!" said the knight. "I'm scared!"

"But it's your job to look after *me*!" said Jake. "Please go and see what's making the noise."

"Only if you come, too," said the knight.

So Jake held the knight's hand
to help him feel braver.

They walked around the dark house
together, looking for the **bump.**

"It's coming from that room," said the knight.

They went inside and saw ...

... a giant shadow in the moonlight!

"It's a big, scary monster!"
said the Night Knight.

Then Jake looked closer.

"It's only Fluffy, my hamster," said Jake. "He's running on his wheel. Go to sleep, Fluffy!"

Soon the house was quiet.

Then something, somewhere, went **rumble grumble!**

"Help!" said the Night Knight. "I'm scared!"

"But it's your job to look after *me*!" said Jake. "Please go and see what's making the noise."

"OK. But only if you come, too," said the knight.

So they walked around the dark house together, looking for the **rumble grumble.**

The **rumble grumble** was coming from Mum's room.

"It's a big, scary monster!" said the knight.

Then Jake looked closer.

"It's only my mum, snoring," said Jake.
"Turn over, Mum!"

Soon the house was quiet again.

Then something, somewhere, went **squeaky creak!**

"Help!" said the Night Knight. "I'm scared!"

He tried to run away but he tripped over his cape.

"Your armour is squeaking," said Jake. "You just need some oil."

Soon the house was quiet again.

"You see?" said Jake. "There's nothing to be scared of."

"Thank you," said the Night Knight. "I feel much braver now."

Jake was very tired. He went back to bed. He said, "Night night," to the Night Knight.

Soon Jake was fast asleep. And the Night Knight looked after him until morning.

Talk about it!

How did I feel at the start of the story?

What was making the rumble grumble noise?

Who do you think was braver, me or the Night Knight?

Spot the difference

Can you spot three differences between these two pictures?

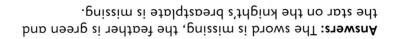

Answers: The sword is missing, the feather is green and the star on the knight's breastplate is missing.

Match the sounds

Draw lines to match the sounds to the things that made them.

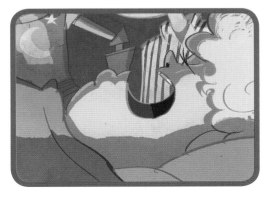

rumble grumble

squeaky creak!

bump

Tomorrow Never Comes

Written by Joanna Nadin

Illustrated by Marion Lindsay

Mabel had nothing to do.

So she went to see Dad.

"Can we go to the circus?"
Mabel asked.

"Maybe tomorrow, Mabel,"
said Dad. "I'm far too busy."

But tomorrow came, and Dad
was still busy.

So Mabel went to see Mum.

"Can we go to the zoo?" she asked.

"Maybe tomorrow, Mabel," said Mum.
"I'm far too busy."

But tomorrow came, and Mum
was still busy.

So Mabel went to see Grandpa.

"Can we go to the beach?" she asked.

"Maybe tomorrow, Mabel," said Grandpa.
"I'm far too busy."

"That's what everyone says!"
Mabel shouted. "But they're always
busy, and tomorrow never comes."

She went up the
stairs to her bedroom
to sulk.

Mabel

As she lay on her bed, Mabel made a plan.

"If everyone is far too busy, I will have adventures all by myself," she said.

First, Mabel swung around her room with four naughty monkeys.

They made a terrible mess of the bookshelves.

Next, she had a tea party with seven silly soldiers.

They made a terrible mess of the carpet.

Then, she did a dance with twelve dangerous dinosaurs.

They made a terrible mess of the walls.

Finally, she had a game of hide-and-seek with fifteen sneaky sheep.

They made a terrible mess of *everything*!

Grandpa knocked on Mabel's door.

"Do you want to go to the beach?" he asked.

"Maybe tomorrow," said Mabel.
"I'm a bit busy."

And she went back to her adventures.

Mum knocked on Mabel's door.

"Do you want to go to the zoo?" she asked.

"Maybe tomorrow," said Mabel.
"I'm a bit busy."

And she went back to her adventures.

Dad knocked on Mabel's door.

"It's an awful mess in here," he said.
"What have you been doing?"

"I've been having adventures," said Mabel.

"Well, I think it's time to tidy up," said Dad.

Mabel smiled.

"Maybe tomorrow," she said. "I'm busy."

Talk about it!

How did I feel at the start of the story?

How did the carpet get messy?

What did I decide to do, when all the grown-ups were too busy?

Odd one out

Draw a circle round the thing that Mabel *didn't* have an adventure with.

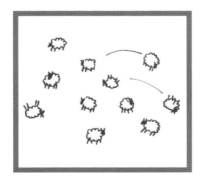

Draw yourself having an adventure with one of your toys.

What are they thinking?

Write what Dad might be thinking when he sees Mabel's messy room.

Write what Mabel might be thinking at the end of the story.